Victorious

30 DAYS IN THE WORD AND PRAYER

CONTRIBUTORS
Pastor Darnell Bryant
Tina Busenitz
Kim Contreras
Rev. Hope Flask
Candy Gibson
Pastor Damon Owens
Rev. Ted Smith

SENIOR EDITORS
Tina Busenitz
Candy Gibson

EDITORS
Kaitlyn Brown
Sharon Browatzke
Rev. Andy Entz
Paula Pust

DESIGN & ARTWORK
Kaitlyn Brown

Dedicated to the beloved community of God—women and men living out their victory in Christ. May you know the power of Christ the Victor in your life, your family, your church, and your community.

A special thanks to the pastors and leaders who graciously gave their time to contribute to this book. Thank you for your passionate love of God's people and His Church.

ABOUT THE COVER ART

In Christian symbolism, the lamb is known as Agnus Dei. This symbol is ancient, appearing within the first 500 years after Jesus' ascension. It represents Christ crucified—Jesus was the sacrificial lamb that brought victory over death, sin, and Satan through His work on the cross and His resurrection. The Agnus Dei is seen throughout the world on stained glass windows of churches, early art, and modern church banners. The Lamb is the gentle leader we follow into victory.

Table of Contents

Foreword

Perhaps the greatest truth emerging from the telling of God's plan in Scripture is concerning His victory in Christ. Humankind's history begins with God's high purpose for His creation, a purpose which Adam and Eve rejected through their rebellion, in the garden of Eden.

From that decisive and sad moment, their sin (alongside our rejection of God's will) has brought misery and pain into the world—alienation, sickness, disease, war, confusion, condemnation, and death. What a tragic tale of disobedience and its horrible effects on human life everywhere!

Even in the face of their transgression, God determined to send a Champion who would deliver us from the curse, delivering us from sin's power, the devil's tyranny, and the power of darkness. He made that promise to Abraham, renewed it with Isaac and Jacob, and prophesied that from Judah's tribe, a king would come to heal the blight of our error and iniquity. A child from David's clan was born of a virgin, Mary, whose name was Jesus (Yeshua), who would save His people from their sins and usher in God's Kingdom of life and light.

How would God execute this grand victory? Amazingly, Jesus won this victory by His death on the cross, the instrument that the Father would use to destroy the devil's works, end the curse, and conquer death. God boldly demonstrated the power of Jesus' triumph by raising Him from the dead on the third day, and setting Him at His right hand as the triumphant Victor over evil.

The prophecy is clear: soon, and very soon, our Lord will return to this earth to complete the mighty work that He began on the cross.

He soon will put the devil down, end the reign of death and sin, and banish all evidence of the curse. And, all of this will be to God's glory alone.

As God's beloved children now through faith in Christ, we have been set free from death's sting, and we celebrate God's victory granted to us through our Lord Jesus Christ. Now that we have been set free, we can be steadfast, immovable, always abounding in the Lord's work, being confident that nothing we do for Christ will be wasted or in vain.

Our theme, *Victorious*, challenges every Christian to live into the whole meaning of Christ's victory for us on the cross. It also gives practical instruction on how we can make that victory come alive in our conduct, character, and relationships. Our prayer for you is that you will discover the power of Christ's victory afresh, and that you will become steadfast and unmoved, abounding in God's work.

Every disciple of Christ has the honor of living in His victory and engaging in His work, knowing that God will bless us in all that we do for Him. Begin your journey today, and may you experience Christ's victory in such a way that your family, friends, and neighbors see what that victory may mean for them.

-Rev. Dr. Don L. Davis
Senior Vice President & Executive Director, TUMI

Introduction

Sometimes we are tempted to measure our life in terms of victories and defeats. Maybe your "defeats" have outnumbered your victories. If this is the case, don't be discouraged. As believers, victorious is our identity in Christ. Christ's work on the cross defeated sin and death and because of this, we live in freedom and victory! Your defeats do not define you—your identity in Christ the Victor does.

1 Corinthians 15.56-58 states: "The sting of death is sin, and the power of sin is the law. But thanks be to God, who gives us the victory through our Lord Jesus Christ. Therefore, my beloved brothers, be steadfast, immovable, always abounding in the work of the Lord, knowing that in the Lord your labor is not in vain."

Our victory in Christ is meant to be lived out to the fullest! So, what does that mean for you?

To help you meditate on what it means to live victoriously, we have divided this book into four themes: Beloved, Steadfast, Abounding, and Your Labor is Not in Vain. Each of these themes expound on what it means to live into our victorious identity.

First and foremost, we are God's beloved. We have victory through Christ because of God's great love for us, and in response to that love, we are called to love one another. Because we are victorious, God calls us to be steadfast in our faith—persevering through trials and struggles. He calls us to serve Him through obedience to His Word. And, finally, we can take courage that our labor is not in vain —God will bring to completion the work He has begun in us and through us.

Each theme contains an introduction written by a church leader/pastor along with a guided prayer as a way for you to think more deeply on the theme.

The devotions in this book are meant to encourage you as you live out your victory in Christ in your home, church, job, and community. Being victorious doesn't mean you won't struggle or encounter trials.

However, it does mean that you can take comfort in the knowledge that Christ loves you and through the Holy Spirit, you will not stay defeated! You may lose some battles, but Christ has won the war!

HOW TO USE THIS BOOK

One of the greatest gifts we have as believers is the ability to spend time in the presence of our Lord. God desires to spend time with us—His beloved children—but the daily pressures and seemingly endless responsibilities we face each day can prevent us from making time with Him a priority. It can seem overwhelming to add ONE MORE THING to our already jam-packed lives.

Sisters and Brothers, we invite you to stop and rest a minute: find a comfortable chair, grab a cup of coffee, take a moment to drop what you're doing, and let the Lord speak to your heart.

The book you hold in your hands contains thirty devotionals. Most of the devotionals are only one page long. If you are in a rush, you can do it in under five minutes. If you have more time, try meditating on the Scripture, re-reading it, and asking the Lord to show you how you can apply His Word to your life.

There are many ways to use this book. Feel free to use it as a small group Bible Study tool—digging into the Scripture passages and discussing the reflection questions. There is a teaching outline in the back of the book that can be used to lead a retreat or preach a sermon series.

Our hope and prayer is that this devotional will bring you closer to our Lord and Savior. Whether you have been studying the Word all your life or just a few weeks, this book is for you!

Tuck this book in your work bag, purse, or car. Let it be a visual reminder that the Lord God of the Universe wants to spend time with YOU.

Tina Busenitz
Director of World Impact Urban Leadership Retreats

1 CORINTHIANS 15.56–58

The sting of death is sin, and the power of sin is the law. But thanks be to God, who gives us the victory through our Lord Jesus Christ. Therefore, my beloved brothers, be steadfast, immovable, always abounding in the work of the Lord, knowing that in the Lord your labor is not in vain.

"The sting of death is sin, and the power of sin is the law. But thanks be to God..." It is always great when there is a BUT in scripture! **But** is the best conjunction in the Bible. Death, sin, and the law do have power, BUT God gives us a way to triumph over them. He gives us Jesus. Jesus is the conjunction we all need.

Through Jesus we are able to be victorious over the sting of death and the punishment of sin. The Jesus conjunction gives way to directions for those who claim victory in His name. We are to remember we are His beloved, we are to be steadfast, abounding in the works of the Lord, and to know our Kingdom labor is not in vain.

REFLECTION QUESTIONS

As you begin this journey into *Victorious*, consider the following questions:

1. What does victory through Jesus look like to you?
2. What does it mean to be beloved?
3. How are you steadfast?
4. What are the works of the Lord that you are to be abounding in?
5. How does it make you feel that your Kingdom labor will not be in vain?

PRAYER EXERCISE

1. Find a space with few distractions. This can be tough when you have children, a roommate, or live with family members. Go for a walk or sit in a car if you need to. Set a timer on your phone and do some breathing exercises. Breathe in deeply and exhale. This will relax your body and begin to focus your mind on Jesus. Breathe in His truth. Breathe out your distractions, worries, and burdens.

2. Ask the Holy Spirit to guide this time with Jesus.

3. Speak one or all of these phrases to Jesus:
   Jesus, You are Victorious!
   Jesus, I am victorious through You.
   Jesus, we are victorious with You (This phrase will lead you to pray for a group of people: family, friends, co-workers, your church community).

4. As distractions come to mind, acknowledge them and refocus your breathing and attention to Jesus and the words you have chosen.

5. If you set a timer and think you need more time, if you can take it, do so. If not, thank Jesus for this time together.

Beloved

In this section, we will reflect on what it means to be God's beloved children and how our victory in Christ enables us to show that love to others—even those who are difficult to love.

"Beloved" is what He calls me. One word that declares that I am seen, known, and loved by the One who created the galaxies and set the moon and stars in place. The very One who formed me, knows me, and calls me His own. It is almost too much for my wearied heart to comprehend. He who spoke creation into existence speaks to me now and breathes life into my broken circumstances. His heart beats off the pages of scripture and beckons me to enter into the dance of creation.

"Be loved," He says to me. His Spirit ministers to mine and calls me to let His love become the balm to my hidden wounds and energy to my tired soul. His love cascades over me and saturates every dry and withered place in my battered heart. He replaces my mourning with joy and crowns me with the beauty of His perfect presence.

"Be Love," He says to me. He calls me up to the Rock that is higher, infuses me with His Light, and tells me to let that Light shine! He wraps me in His garment of love and sets me apart for divine work. I am called to be love in the hardest and darkest places. Not eventually, not someday, but to be love right now; so that others may know what it means to Be Loved.

Rev. Hope Flask

PRAYER EXERCISE

1. Find a space with few distractions. This can be tough when you have children, a roommate, or live with family members. Go for a walk or sit in a car if you need to. Set a timer on your phone and do some breathing exercises. Breathe in deeply, and exhale. This will relax your body and begin to focus your mind on Jesus. Breathe in His truth. Breathe out your distractions, worries, and burdens.

2. Ask the Holy Spirit to guide this time with Jesus.

3. Speak one or all of these phrases to Jesus:
   Jesus, you are the Beloved!
   Jesus, I am the Beloved.
   Jesus, we are all the Beloved (This phrase will lead you to pray for a group of people: family, friends, co-workers, your church community).

4. As distractions come to mind, acknowledge them and refocus your breathing and attention to Jesus and the words you have chosen.

5. If you set a timer and think you need more time, if you can take it, do so. If not, thank Jesus for this time together.

1 JOHN 3.2

See what kind of love the Father has given to us, that we should be called children of God; and so we are. The reason why the world does not know us is that it did not know him. Beloved, we are God's children now, and what we will be has not yet appeared; but we know that when he appears we shall be like him, because we shall see him as he is.

God is King and Creator of the Universe. But He is also our Father—our Daddy. The King of Kings calls us His beloved and precious children! He lavishes His love on us. Maybe you didn't grow up with loving parents and so understanding this kind of love can be difficult. When you have doubts, remind yourself who you are: A beloved child of the King. Let His love transform you from the inside out.

Don't worry if you don't see changes in your life right away. God's love will surely refine us and make us more like Christ. With His help, we can experience victory over the bondage of sin and live more freely. And when our time has come to pass from this world to the next, we can be assured that we will meet God face to face. What a joy that will be!

REFLECTION QUESTIONS

1. Do you struggle with seeing yourself as a beloved child of God?
2. How is God's love transforming the way you think and behave?

PRAYER

Take a few moments and meditate on the lyrics as a prayer to God.

"Who You Say I Am"
Hillsong Worship

Who am I that the highest King would welcome me?
I was lost, but He brought me in
Oh His love for me
Oh His love for me
Who the Son sets free
Oh, is free indeed
I'm a child of God, yes, I am

Free at last, He has ransomed me
His grace runs deep
While I was a slave to sin, Jesus died for me
Yes, He died for me
Who the Son sets free
Oh is free indeed

I am chosen, not forsaken
I am who You say I am
You are for me, not against me
I am who You say I am
I am chosen, not forsaken

Amen

EPHESIANS 5.1–2

Therefore be imitators of God, as beloved children. And walk in love, as Christ loved us and gave himself up for us, a fragrant offering and sacrifice to God.

As God's precious and beloved children, we are called to be imitators of Him. Yikes! That seems like a tall order. It is easy to get discouraged and overwhelmed when we contemplate how to be like Christ. We are constantly aware of our own failings and limitations. However, the second sentence in the passage sums up the main command. We are called to walk in love as Christ loved us. When we love others as Christ loved us, we come as close as we can to imitating God.

It isn't about trying to do a bunch of good works for the sake of doing good works. Galatians 5:14 says, "For the whole law is fulfilled in one word: 'You shall love your neighbor as yourself.'" This kind of love is not a feeling; it is an action. Victorious living means reaching out to your enemies and to those who are hard to love. Build others up. Be quick to share an encouraging word. Be like Christ. Love others.

REFLECTION QUESTIONS

1. What does "loving others" look like in your life?
2. What's a barrier you face to loving others?

PRAYER

Dear Father,
I admit that it can be overwhelming to love others as You love me.
Breathe Your love into my life that I might freely give it to others.
Even when it is tough, give me the strength to love my fellow sisters
and brothers. Thank You for sacrificing Your life so that I can live
victoriously—both here and in eternity.
Amen

GENESIS 16.13

So she called the name of the Lord who spoke to her, "You are a God of seeing," for she said, "Truly here I have seen him who looks after me."

Did you ever get separated from your parent in the grocery store as a child? Do you remember the sense of panic and fear as you searched each aisle for that familiar face? Then, after what seemed like an eternity, you see your mom or dad.

You lock eyes with them and realize they see you too, and you are filled with relief and a sense of safety. Our Heavenly Father never loses sight of us—even when we lose sight of Him. When we feel lost, He sees us.

He looks upon our distress and extends His love and compassion to us. Just like Hagar, we can call on the Lord and know He hears us. Hagar was a concubine of Abraham who was banished from her home after Abraham's wife grew jealous of her pregnancy (Genesis 16).

In the desert, without provision or hope, she cried out to the Lord. God saved her and promised that He would provide for her and her son, and He did. We can take comfort that we are God's beloved children, and He sees us and cares for us.

REFLECTION QUESTIONS

1. Can you recall a difficult time in your life when you sensed God's presence? How did you feel?
2. Currently, are there situations in your life that are causing you distress? Take time to tell the Lord what is worrying you.

PRAYER

Heavenly Father,
I know that You see me right now. You know my thoughts and You
know my circumstances. You understand my fears, insecurities, and
the difficult things I am experiencing. As I go throughout my day,
may I be reminded of Your love and provision for me. Give me the
wisdom and strength to tackle the hard things in my life. I praise
Your compassion and provision for me.
Amen

JUDE 1.20-21

But you, dear friends, by building yourselves up in your most holy faith and praying in the Holy Spirit, keep yourselves in God's love as you wait for the mercy of our Lord Jesus Christ to bring you to eternal life.

Much of life is a practice in perseverance. We persevere through trials, physical suffering, and tragic events. Perseverance is not passive. It requires us to bolster our faith through prayer. Perseverance requires us to keep going even when the road is difficult.

But, beloved, we can take heart! Even during life's hardships, we can stand in victory. As God's dearly loved children we are sustained through the Holy Spirit and the love of our Heavenly Father. And we know that this present life will eventually pass away—along with sin, strife, tears, and suffering. Then, we will be united with Christ in eternal life where our perseverance will be rewarded.

REFLECTION QUESTIONS

1. What areas of your life require perseverance?
2. Take a moment to give your struggles to God and ask for the Holy Spirit's strength as you persevere.

PRAYER

Heavenly Father,
I come before You with my struggles and burdens. Through the power of Your Holy Spirit, give me the strength I need to persevere. Through these trials, let my faith grow deeper. Make me aware of Your presence in my life and Your unfailing love for me. Thank you for the eternal life You promised to those who believe.
Amen

COLOSSIANS 3.12

Put on then, as God's chosen ones, holy and beloved, compassionate hearts, kindness, humility, meekness, and patience.

It is quite amazing to think that the only Son of God came down from heaven to live life as a humble carpenter. He was born in a stable and He grew up in Nazareth—a town known for its bad reputation.

His life and ministry did not look like the powerful people of His time—kings, rulers and religious leaders. His victory did not involve wielding His power for personal fame and glory.

Instead, He became a servant. He showed compassion to women and children. He healed the broken and sick. He washed the feet of His disciples. And in the greatest act of love and humility, He died on a cross, defeating sin and death—the ultimate victory.

Because we are God's chosen and beloved people, we are called to follow Christ's example. The verse commands us to "put on" these attributes. When we wear something, it is constantly with us. As long as it is on, it is attached to us. Let us attach ourselves to compassion, kindness, humility, meekness, and patience.

REFLECTION QUESTIONS

1. How does Christ's example challenge your perceptions about leadership and power?
2. How would your daily life change if you focused on integrating compassion, kindness, meekness, and patience?

PRAYER

Heavenly Father,
When I am tempted to be unkind, impatient, and prideful, give me
the strength to follow Your example. Thank You for showing me
the compassion and kindness I didn't deserve. As I seek to do Your
will in my family, job, ministry, and community, may I lead through
serving others.
Amen

1 JOHN 4.7–8

Beloved, let us love one another, for love is from God, and whoever loves has been born of God and knows God. Anyone who does not love does not know God, because God is love.

When we look at social media or watch the news, we see people taking sides. And not only taking sides but spewing hate toward the opposing side. It is natural to love those who are like us—who think like us and share our views. It is easy to love those who love us back. The Bible is clear on who we are to love: everyone.

This does not mean that we are called to be in relationship with people who are toxic or harmful to us (love allows for setting appropriate boundaries). It does mean that our thoughts, words, and actions should convey the love God has shown us.

Remember that Christ asked God to forgive those who crucified Him (Luke 23.34)! If we want to truly know God and live in victory, we can't pick and choose to whom we show kindness and compassion.

REFLECTION QUESTIONS

1. Who do you have trouble loving?
2. How have you experienced God's love in your own life?
3. When you recognize God's love in your own life, how do you begin to view others?

PRAYER

Our Father, here I am, at Your disposal, Your child, to use me to continue Your loving the world, by giving Jesus to me and through me, to each other and to the world. Let us pray for each other that we allow Jesus to love in us and through us with the love with which His Father loves us.
Amen
-Mother Teresa[1]

[1] *Encyclopedia of Prayer and Praise*, 2004, Edited by Mark Water, Peabody, Massachusetts, Hendrickson Publishing

Steadfast

In this section we will reflect and meditate on what it means to be steadfast in our faith and how living out our victory in Christ requires perseverance, hope, and confidence in the Lord.

I love the movie *Harriet*! It captures the story of Harriet Tubman, a woman who was STEADFAST. She wasn't formally educated. People who met her couldn't believe she was the woman who ran the Underground Railroad; nothing about her physical appearance or demeanor stood out as exceptional. She even suffered from fainting spells that would come over her, and she could do nothing but succumb—often at the worst possible times—yet she was never captured.

None of this stopped her from her determination to lead her people to freedom. She was relentless in this pursuit, and her trust was firmly in the Lord as she took to this task. She had no particular qualifications or permission. What she had was a deeply held faith that those created in God's image should have the freedom to live and be all they could be and a determination to make that happen.

Harriet's steadfastness didn't begin with that first group of enslaved people she led on the Underground Railroad. It started in the field and kitchen, where she worked and dreamed of freedom. It grew in her heart as she talked with the Lord and sang songs with other enslaved people around her.

Like Harriet, how are you becoming unmovable, faithful, loyal, determined as you listen to what the Lord is calling you to do at this time? Where are you learning to be steadfast? It may not be flashy or popular; it may seem like the least likely place to grow for the task the Lord is putting in your heart. Others may even shake their head in disbelief that you have these thoughts.

As you enter this time, listen carefully; let Jesus' words nurture your life and tend to your soul. Let it pour courage into the places where the Spirit shapes you for the impossible work you're uniquely created to influence and lead.

Ministry Developer Kim Contreras

PRAYER EXERCISE

1. Find a space with few distractions. This can be tough when you have children, a roommate, or live with family members. Go for a walk or sit in a car if you need to. Set a timer on your phone and do some breathing exercises. Breathe in deeply, and exhale. This will relax your body and begin to focus your mind on Jesus. Breathe in His truth. Breathe out your distractions, worries, and burdens.

2. Ask the Holy Spirit to guide this time with Jesus.

3. Speak one or all of these phrases to Jesus:
   Jesus, You are Steadfast!
   Jesus, I am becoming steadfast.
   Jesus, may we be steadfast (This phrase will lead you to pray for a group of people: family, friends, co-workers, your church community).

4. As distractions come to mind, acknowledge them and refocus your breathing and attention to Jesus and the words you have chosen.

5. If you set a timer and think you need more time, if you can take it, do so. If not, thank Jesus for this time together.

HEBREWS 10.23–25

Let us hold fast the confession of our hope without wavering, for he who promised is faithful. And let us consider how to stir up one another to love and good works, not neglecting to meet together, as is the habit of some, but encouraging one another, and all the more as you see the Day drawing near.

Do you know how to hold onto hope? How do we grasp this intangible idea? The writer of Hebrews implies that one way to hold onto hope is to do it in community.

When a believer does not sway from hope, God's faithfulness meets them in the hoping. This meeting can be through the community of those who follow Jesus. Together it is easier to hope. Together we can be reminded that God is present, and we can share testimony of God's active participation in our lives. Together we can do good in the world, and encourage each other, because hope in the victorious resurrected Savior is worth holding on to.

There is much to let go of in this life—hatred, bitterness, anger, sin—but hope is worth clutching tightly. Walking with others who hope in the Lord is a great joy. So keep gathering; keep doing good; and keep hoping.

REFLECTION QUESTIONS

1. How do you hold onto hope?
2. Who in your life encourages you to hope in the Lord, do good deeds, and get in community?

PRAYER

Father,
Surround me with those who do good in your name, those who
seek the Kingdom, and those who place their hope firmly in You.
Bring people to my mind right now who follow after you (*silence
for 1 minute*). Thank You for (*name those who came to mind*). May I
encourage them this week as we place our hope in You.
Amen

ISAIAH 26.3-4

You keep him in perfect peace
whose mind is stayed on you,
because he trusts in you.
Trust in the LORD forever,
for the LORD GOD is an everlasting rock.

Have you ever been to a lake first thing in the morning, as the sun is rising? It is often like a sheet of glass, still and quiet. The fish are still sleeping and the fishermen are just starting to drop their lines in. It is peaceful and grand. The perfect peace of the Lord is even better than the lake at dawn.

When our minds are steadfast on Him, He can calm the anxiety; He can comfort the broken; He can hold all the pieces, and give us peace. "Steadfast" is an old-fashioned word. We do not use it much today. But it is a really deep word.

To be steadfast means to be resolutely or dutifully firm and unwavering. When our minds are steadfast on the Lord, we are beyond sure of His ways. We obey and believe in the Word, and we stand on His truth no matter what others say we should do.

When we are steadfast in the Rock Eternal, He gives us the perfect peace we need to journey through life. He gives us rest at the still lake when we need it.

REFLECTION QUESTION

1. When was a time you felt the perfect peace of the Lord?

PRAYER

I wait now in silence, Lord, that the peace may spring up and the anxiety dissipate.
Sit in silence (2-10 minutes).
May Your steadfast light continually overcome my darkness.
Amen
-Adapted from "A Prayer of Stillness"[2]

[2]*Prayers from the Heart*, 1994, Richard Foster, New York, New York, HarperCollins Publishers

2 THESSALONIANS 3.5

May the Lord direct your hearts into the love of God and into the steadfastness of Christ. (NASB)

When Christians pray, something interesting happens. Actually, many amazing things happen, but one of the things that happens is the Lord changes the heart of the one praying. When we pray, we change. God uses our requests, petitions, and praises to alter our desires, will, and adoration.

When we are open to His direction, we change. We become more like Him. We become more loving. This is a love that is freely given to all with whom we come into contact. The love of God is no joke. It is attractive, free, and keeps no records of wrongs. It looks vastly different from what movies, books, and TV give us.

With God's love there is no manipulation or ulterior motives; it is a love that is given to all because we are made in His image.

Not only does the love of God change us, but it directs us to the steadfastness of Christ. Jesus stayed on mission. He was unwavering.

We, too, can be steadfast, steadfast to the victorious message of reconciliation that was fulfilled in Jesus' death and resurrection. We are to be unwavering in this truth. Our hearts are to focus on Jesus and His victory over the grave.

REFLECTION QUESTIONS

1. How has the Lord changed your heart in times of prayer?
2. How do you want to become more like Christ?

PRAYER

Lord,
You know what I desire, but I desire it only if it is your will
that I should have it. If it is not your will, good Lord, do not be
displeased, for my will is to do your will.
Amen
-Lady Julian of Norwich[2]

2 TIMOTHY 2.15

Do your best to present yourself to God as one approved, a worker who has no need to be ashamed, rightly handling the word of truth.

When we go before the Lord, can we say that we rightly handled the Word of truth? Have we studied it in community? There is an old saying that is used in many Christian circles: "Have you put flesh on it?" Have you put flesh on the Word of truth? That means that you have taken the words of Jesus and biblical authors and put them into practice in your life. You have taken the words and moved them to actions. We handle the Word not just by studying, or sitting under good teaching; we handle it by doing what it says.

We can present ourselves to the Lord, fully unashamed and approved when we handle the Word correctly.

REFLECTION QUESTIONS

1. Is there a passage in scripture you have a hard time acting on? If so, what passage is it?
2. How do you correctly handle the Word of truth?

PRAYER

Lord,
Help me put flesh on the Word of truth. Allow me to not only study but also act. May I be a walking example of Your truth. May my obedience draw people to You.
Amen

HEBREWS 10.35-36

Therefore do not throw away your confidence, which has a great reward. For you have need of endurance, so that when you have done the will of God you may receive what is promised.

It is easy to lose confidence when things do not work out for the millionth time; when that little bit of savings needs to go to an unforeseen car repair; when that special someone does not seem interested; when layoffs come knocking at your door. Confidence in the Lord and His ways can be easily thrown away when it is hard to see Him at work.

Confidence is easy when things are going well, but how do we stay steadfast when there are hiccups? This scripture is helpful; when we are confident in the will of God, His promises meet us in His timing. When our confidence is slipping, we must look to God's truth and remember that He has a plan, and if we are walking in His will, He will not withhold His promises from us.

What are these promises? The scriptures tell us that:
- He will never leave you or forsake you (Psalm 27.10).
- Nothing will separate us from the love of God that is in Jesus Christ (Romans 8.38-39).
- He has redeemed you and summoned you by name; you are His (Isaiah 43.1).

And these three Scriptures are just scratching the surface of God's promises. When we place our confidence in Him, His ways, and His truth, He is gracious and overwhelmingly good.

REFLECTION QUESTIONS

1. What is a biblical promise you hold onto when life is hard?
2. When have you needed confidence in the Lord?

PRAYER

Lord,
When the stress of life consumes my thoughts
Remind me that
You will never leave me nor forsake me
When the distance seems too far and I feel too alone
Remind me that
Nothing can separate me from your love
When the pain of being sinned against makes me forget who I am
Remind me that
You have summoned me by name and I am yours
Amen

2 PETER 3.17–18

You therefore, beloved, knowing this beforehand, take care that you are not carried away with the error of lawless people and lose your own stability. But grow in the grace and knowledge of our Lord and Savior Jesus Christ. To him be the glory both now and to the day of eternity. Amen.

There is a show on PBS called *Antiques Roadshow*. People bring their antiques, collectables, and family heirlooms to be appraised by experts. The men and women who do the appraisals are in the top of their fields. They know not only the value but also if the item is authentic or a fake. They know the fakes because they have extensively studied the real thing.

We, as followers of Christ, have to be so immersed in God's truth and steadfast to His ways that when false teachings come at us we are guarded against them.

We must know the truth so deeply that when false teachings, fake prophets, or lies come into our faith communities we can reject them, because we know what is being said is not of the Lord.

We will know a fake because we are surrounded by truth. That truth will allow us to grow in grace and knowledge. Grace will help us when we mess up and knowledge will allow us to keep from messing up again.

REFLECTION QUESTION

1. How do you guard against false teaching and bad theology?

PRAYER

Father,
Give me a discerning ear, a guarded heart, and a sharp mind.
Surround me with your truth and with those who know You better
than I do, so that I may grow in Your ways. Grant me grace and
knowledge so that I will be more like You.
Amen

Abounding

**BECAUSE WE ARE VICTORIOUS, WE ARE ABOUNDING
IN THE WORKS OF THE LORD**

———————

*In this section, we will look at what are the works of the Lord and
how living victoriously means serving others, showing love and
concern for the poor, and making disciples.*

JOHN 13.34

*A new commandment I give to you, that you love one another: just as
I have loved you, you also are to love one another.*

In John's gospel, Jesus reminds us of the importance of keeping
the main thing, the main thing—knowing that whatever work
we do for the Lord has eternal value. If it is true that without love
we are nothing, then it may also be true that loveless works and
loveless prayers produce absolutely nothing (1 Corinthians 13.1-3).
Everything we do for the Lord has eternal value.

God has enlisted you into His army for a reason and a purpose,
and that greater purpose is more significant than what you can see
or imagine. As a disciple of Jesus, it is our responsibility to stand
up, come alongside our brothers and sisters, and push back against
injustice as we share the illuminating light of the gospel of Jesus
Christ with love.

Jesus Christ is not only our Lord, but He's also our example. Jesus
extended His heart and love to a woman caught in adultery. The
Lord showed mercy, compassion, and empathy to the woman in her

shame while urging her to go and sin no more (John 8.9-11).

It's easy to be critical, judgmental, and insensitive. As the Church, we are quick to cast judgment and shame others who have sinned. Guilt, shame, and condemnation are things the enemy will use to keep people trapped in a confused state of feeling undeserving of God's love.

It is only when the love of God builds a bridge to wounded and broken hearts that healing and repentance can begin. Let us do our part by keeping the main thing, the main thing. Let us live victoriously by doing our work for the Lord with love and compassion.

Pastor Damon Owens

PRAYER

Lord Jesus,
You have commanded me to love others the same way You love me, though I may not receive the same love in return. Give me eyes and a heart to love others who are broken, and help me be intentional to reach out and share Your love with them.
In Jesus Name, Amen

PRAYER EXERCISE

1. Find a space with few distractions. This can be tough when you have children, a roommate, or live with family members. Go for a walk or sit in a car if you need to. Set a timer on your phone and do some breathing exercises. Breathe in deeply, and exhale. This will relax your body and begin to focus your mind on Jesus. Breathe in His truth. Breathe out your distractions, worries, and burdens.

2. Ask the Holy Spirit to guide this time with Jesus.

3. Speak one or all of these phrases to Jesus:
   Jesus, You are at work!
   Jesus, I am partnering with you.
   Jesus, we are working alongside You (This phrase will lead you to pray for a group of people: family, friends, co-workers, your church community).

4. As distractions come to mind, acknowledge them and refocus your breathing and attention to Jesus and the words you have chosen.

5. If you set a timer and think you need more time, if you can take it, do so. If not, thank Jesus for this time together.

JAMES 1.27

Religion that is pure and undefiled before God the Father is this: to visit orphans and widows in their affliction, and to keep oneself unstained from the world.

How do we keep our eyes focused on God? We take care of the vulnerable. In James' day the orphans and the widows were the epitome of vulnerable populations. Today they still are! How many times have we seen local news stories about the elderly being scammed? Or a story about a child in foster care being abused?

James tells us that God desires for the people of the Kingdom to care for, watch out for, house, and seek justice on behalf of vulnerable people.

After James tells us how to care for others, he instructs us as to how we take care of ourselves. James says we need to be "unpolluted by the world." Those are big words. Pollution is not good; it is the root of many problems. A bit of contaminant can pollute the entire water system! As participants in the Kingdom we must not allow pollutants into our lives.

We need to purify our hearts and stay clear from the pollution that comes from the earthly lust for power, political parties, wealth, racism—people of the Kingdom are to stay focused on being set apart and holy. We are not to look like "the world," we are to follow Jesus and His ways of forgiveness, love, and justice.

This is not an easy way to live, but it is pure and faultless in the eyes of God.

REFLECTION QUESTIONS

1. What pollutants do you need to allow the Lord to purify?
2. How do you care for the orphans and the widows?

PRAYER

O Most High, Glorious God, enlighten the darkness of my heart and give me
A right faith, A certain hope
And a perfect love, understanding and knowledge,
O Lord, That I may carry out your holy and true command.
Amen
-Francis of Assisi[2]

MATTHEW 28.18–20

And Jesus came and said to them, "All authority in heaven and on earth has been given to me. Go therefore and make disciples of all nations, baptizing them in the name of the Father and of the Son and of the Holy Spirit, teaching them to observe all that I have commanded you. And behold, I am with you always, to the end of the age."

The words of Jesus are often too familiar. They have been preached from pulpits, tattooed on bodies, and painted on signs for sale at your local Hobby Lobby, and yet we don't really know them at all. Or maybe we just think they are nice ideas, but actually doing them can be messy.

Jesus tells those gathered to "Go and make disciples." Discipleship is messy. It was for Jesus. He spent years with the 12, living with them, instructing them, discipling them. He had one who denied Him three times, one who constantly doubted, one who straight up betrayed Him—discipleship is not easy. It involves humans, so it is messy, and yet we are called to follow Jesus' example and walk alongside people in the mess and point them towards a Jesus life.

Jesus then tells those gathered to baptize. This is giving the opportunity to publicly proclaim, "I'm with Jesus." This declaration comes with a way to live—a way that Jesus tells His followers to live.

Jesus commands us to love our enemies (Matthew 5.44–46), be reconciled to one another (Matthew 5.23–25), seek the Kingdom of God (Matthew 6.33), welcome the poor (Luke 14.12–14), and so much more.

Followers of Jesus will look different because our love for Jesus will overflow to those around us, because Jesus is with us. He is present in our discipleship, in our baptizing, and in our obedience.

REFLECTION QUESTIONS

1. Have you ever been part of messy discipleship? How did it change your life?
2. What are some of the commands of Jesus we need to obey when following Him?

PRAYER

Father,
May the world see Your Son through me. May they glimpse the Kingdom because of my love for Jesus and my following of Your ways. Open my eyes to see those longing for hope, and open my mouth to tell them of Your redeeming love.
Amen

JOHN 13.34–35

A new commandment I give to you, that you love one another: just as I have loved you, you also are to love one another. By this all people will know that you are my disciples, if you have love for one another.

The late theologian Francis Schaeffer wrote an amazing little book called, *The Mark of a Christian*. In this booklet he talks about how throughout history Christians have tried to set themselves apart by special dress or haircuts or symbols—none of these are bad, but Jesus desires for His followers to be marked by love.

> *Notice that what He says here is not a statement or a fact. It is a command which includes a condition: By this all men will know that you are my disciples, if you love one another. And if this is involved, if you obey, you will wear the badge that Christ gave. But since this is a command, it can be violated. The point: while it is possible to be a Christian without showing the mark; if we expect non-Christians to know that we are Christians, we must show the mark. Speaking to the church some years later, the same John who wrote the account above says: This is the message you heard from the beginning: We should love one another. (1 John 3:11) John in effect says: Don't forget this… don't forget this! This command was given to us by Christ while He was still on earth. This is to be your mark.*

This command is not easy. It can be hard to love people, but when we choose to love others we show the mark of following Jesus. This love is a work of the Lord in your life, and in the lives of others. Be diligent; be marked by love.

REFLECTION QUESTIONS

1. When was it hard for you to show God's love to someone?
2. What, in your life, would change if you were to live a life focused on loving others?

PRAYER

O my God, let me walk in the way of love which knoweth not how to seek self in anything whatsoever. But what love must it be? It must be an ardent love, a pure love, a courageous love, a love of charity, a humble love, and a constant love. O Lord, give this love into my soul, that I may never more live nor breathe but out of a most pure love of Thee, my All and only God.
Amen
-Dame Gertrude More[2]

LUKE 10.25-37

"Which of these three, do you think, proved to be a neighbor to the man who fell among the robbers?" He said, "The one who showed him mercy." And Jesus said to him, "You go, and do likewise."

Imagine being one of these "experts." Put yourself in those shoes. You are an expert in the law. You have been listening to Jesus all day, and you finally have worked up a question to test Him. With great confidence you stand and put your question before Jesus. There is a feeling one gets when they have won the argument, a smugness—that is how you feel. You have found the loophole.

BUT JESUS. Jesus interacts with you and begins to share a story. A story of privilege, assault, and love. This story is about a road you travel often. You have walked to Jericho in your robes, knowing no one will touch you because of your standing in the community. You know of the robbers. You place yourself in Jesus' story and see the hurt man.

As an "expert in the law" you have a tight schedule to keep, so you hurry along. Maybe for the rest of the day somewhere in the back of your mind you wonder how that naked, half-dead man is doing. Maybe the woulda, shoulda, coulda mess with your mind. But you had a schedule to keep.

Jesus keeps the story rolling with the most unlikely hero—a Samaritan. Not only does this man help the naked, half-dead man, he clothes him, pays for his lodging and medical care. You are now becoming embarrassed that the lowest in society is the hero. You are now the villain, and a Samaritan is the victor.

And Jesus turns the question back to you, "Which of these three do you think was a neighbor to the man who fell into the hands of robbers?" You answer, sit down, and Jesus tells you to be more like the lowly, outcast Samaritan.

REFLECTION QUESTIONS

1. Why is it easier to see yourself in the Good Samaritan than the other characters in the parable?
2. How do we become more like the Good Samaritan and less like the other characters?

PRAYER

Today, O Lord, I'm listening to the proclamation of the Word. Help me to listen as much with the heart and the will as I do with the head.
Amen
-Richard Foster[2]

LUKE 3.7–14

And the crowds asked him, "What then shall we do?"
And he answered them, "Whoever has two tunics is to share with him
who has none, and whoever has food is to do likewise."
Tax collectors also came to be baptized and said to him, "Teacher,
what shall we do?"
And he said to them, "Collect no more than you are authorized to do."
Soldiers also asked him, "And we, what shall we do?" And he said
to them, "Do not extort money from anyone by threats or by false
accusation, and be content with your wages."

John the Baptist comes out of the wilderness with the message of, "Repent!" This message is just as relevant today as it was then. John is showing them and us a new way. He is telling them and us to love others. Luke 3.11 says, "Anyone who has two shirts should share with the one who has none, and anyone who has food should do the same." The repentance he speaks of includes caring for the poor.

When the tax collectors came to be baptized, they asked "Teacher, what should we do?"

And John said, "Don't collect any more than you are required to." His repentance included equitable justice. We must examine our definition of justice. When we turn from the injustice of the empire, are we turning to equitable and fair business practices?

And when the soldiers asked him, "And what should we do?" He replied, "Don't extort money and don't accuse people falsely—be content with your pay." His repentance included fair and just systems of power. Does ours?

Are we hearing John the Baptist? He was rooting out systemic injustice with the word "repent." He was calling this crowd to deny themselves and see the worth in others and to preserve the dignity of those in lower economic and power structures. This is the repentance we enter into. This is the victorious way of Jesus.

REFLECTION QUESTIONS

1. What do you think of John the Baptist's words?
2. How is your definition of repentance different from John's?

PRAYER

Stir me, O Lord, to care; for a world that is lost and dying, for values that are rejected and scorned, for enemies that hate and malign me. Amen
-Richard Foster[2]

MARK 10.17–27

And Jesus, looking at him, loved him, and said to him, "You lack one thing: go, sell all that you have and give to the poor, and you will have treasure in heaven; and come, follow me." Disheartened by the saying, he went away sorrowful, for he had great possessions.

The story of the Rich Young Ruler is a tough one. Why must this young man sell all of his belongings? How come he is not told to pray a "simple" prayer and be saved? Why does Jesus ask this of him?

The Rich Young Ruler was asked to sell his belongings in order to rid himself of his gods and idols. His stuff was his priority. His stuff was his identity. Jesus asked him to prioritize the King and the Kingdom, and to do that he needed to let go of his idols and place Jesus on the throne of his life. He was not interested in a new life. The Rich Young Ruler walked away from Jesus unable to part with his stuff.

Following Jesus is not just a simple prayer—it is a lifestyle of uprooting idols and false gods while reorienting our thoughts, hearts, and actions toward Jesus. Followers of Jesus look like Jesus. The Rich Young Ruler looked like those in his social kingdom. Jesus calls for us to look like those in His Kingdom—the lowly, the poor, the foolish in the eyes of the world. For some of us this may be a radical change, and for some of us it might not be worth it.

REFLECTION QUESTIONS

1. How do you think the disciples felt when the Rich Young Ruler walked away?
2. What gods and idols do you need to lay down for the sake of the Kingdom?

PRAYER

Today, O Lord, I say YES!
to you,
to life,
to your Kingdom,
to your ways,
to all that is true, and good, and beautiful.
Amen
-adapted from *A Prayer of Covenant* by Richard Foster[2]

Your Labor is Not in Vain

————

In this section, we will study what it looks like for us to fully commit ourselves to serving the Lord—emboldened by the knowledge that we are victorious and nothing we do for the Lord is in vain.

Beloved, Christ is our Victor and Victory. "The sting of death is sin…But thanks be to God! He gives us the victory through our Lord Jesus Christ" (1 Corinthians 15.56-57). Let's take a moment to praise our perfect Father for His perfect plan of salvation and reconciliation through Christ Jesus our Lord. God saved you by His grace when you believed.

And you can't take credit for this; it is a gift from God. Salvation is not a reward for the good things we have done, so none of us can boast about it (Ephesians 2.8-9). The same God that destroyed Pharaoh's army is the same God fighting your battles. Use your weapons of praise and thanksgiving to be encouraged that your victory is in Jesus' name! Jesus openly defeated the father of lies on that hill called Golgotha.

Therefore, Satan, the enemy of our souls (mind, will, and emotions) would love to trick us into believing that we cannot be delivered, healed, or freed from his plan or our past. The devil wants to derail you, distract you, and shame you out of your identity in Christ, as well as your labor in love. God wants you to be encouraged as He has created you for good works.

Truth be told, serving the King is one of the hardest things you will ever do. Things will get difficult, and you will be inconvenienced; you will run out of strength and want to quit. Be encouraged; if you don't quit, you will reap the eternal things you have sowed. As you serve God with pure hearts and hands, allow the Holy Spirit to continuously remind you that everything you do, you do unto the Lord.

Pastor Darnell Bryant

PRAYER EXERCISE

1. Find a space with few distractions. This can be tough when you have children, a roommate, or live with family members. Go for a walk or sit in a car if you need to. Set a timer on your phone and do some breathing exercises. Breathe in deeply, and exhale. This will relax your body and begin to focus your mind on Jesus. Breathe in His truth. Breathe out your distractions, worries, and burdens.

2. Ask the Holy Spirit to guide this time with Jesus.

3. Speak one or all of these phrases to Jesus:
Jesus, Your Kingdom is here!
Jesus, I am a Kingdom servant.
Jesus, we are Kingdom heirs (This phrase will lead you to pray for a group of people: family, friends, co-workers, your church community).

4. As distractions come to mind, acknowledge them and refocus your breathing and attention to Jesus and the words you have chosen.

5. If you set a timer and think you need more time, if you can take it, do so. If not, thank Jesus for this time together.

EPHESIANS 2.8–10

For by grace you have been saved through faith. And this is not your own doing; it is the gift of God, not a result of works, so that no one may boast. For we are His workmanship, created in Christ Jesus for good works, which God prepared beforehand, that we should walk in them.

In the passage above, the word "work," in some form, appears three times. The first time, God is making it clear to us that the gift of salvation cannot be earned by our good works. Salvation is a gracious gift from God. The second mention of "work" is in reference to our identity.

To be clear, our good works are not our identity—it is the fact that we are God's workmanship. The definition of workmanship is an object that is skillfully crafted. God has skillfully crafted us with unique gifts in order that we might serve Him and live victoriously.

The third "work" is referring to the work of serving the Lord. From the very beginning God knew who you would become, and He desires to use all of you (the good, the bad, and the ugly) to further His Kingdom through good works. The trials you have experienced have not been in vain. The God of the Universe created you for His purposes.

REFLECTION QUESTIONS

1. Do you struggle at times with the knowledge that you can't earn your salvation—that it is a gift from God?
2. What gifts has God given you that you are using to serve Him?

PRAYER

Teach us, gracious Lord, to begin our deeds with reverence, to go on with obedience, and then finish them with love; and then to wait patiently in hope, and with cheerful confidence to look up to You, whose promises are faithful and rewards infinite; through Jesus Christ.
Amen
-George Hickes[1]

GALATIANS 6.9–10

And let us not grow weary of doing good, for in due season we will reap, if we do not give up. So then, as we have opportunity, let us do good to everyone, and especially to those who are of the household of faith.

It is easy to get overwhelmed and exhausted in the midst of serving God. Sometimes our weariness is due to a lack of taking care of our physical bodies and emotional health. If that's the case, we need to stop and take stock of how we can better care for ourselves.

Other times, our weariness comes because we don't feel like the ministry we are doing, whether it is to our families, churches, or communities, is making a difference. We planted the seeds, but we see no fruit. Don't give up!

Keep ministering to your lost children, keep discipling the new believers in your church, and keep showing compassion to the lost. Victorious living means that we do good to everyone with the belief that God will use it for His glory, even if we can't always see it.

REFLECTION QUESTIONS

1. At what point in your life have you experienced weariness in serving the Lord?
2. How did God encourage you during those moments of weariness?

PRAYER

Dear God,
I confess that at times I do not feel like serving others or doing good. Sometimes I feel like what I am doing has no impact on the Kingdom. Please give me faith to know that my labor is not in vain and that You will bring to completion the work I have started. Help me to remain strong and not give up.
Amen

COLOSSIANS 3.23–24

Whatever you do, work heartily, as for the Lord and not for men, knowing that from the Lord you will receive the inheritance as your reward. You are serving the Lord Christ.

Have you ever worked really hard for something and someone else got the credit? Or perhaps God has gifted you to work behind the scenes, and, therefore, you rarely get the accolades and applause that those serving "up front" receive. It's human nature to want to be recognized and receive awards and promotions.

However, too often we associate victory with personal gain and recognition from people. God calls us to do our work to the best of our abilities—not to please others—but to do it unto the Lord. It doesn't matter whether we are pastors, teachers, plumbers or artists; we should do our work as if we are doing it for the Lord—because we are!

Our reward is our inheritance from the Lord—eternal life. Our reward is also living victoriously. Whether or not we gain earthly rewards, we can enjoy the freedom and peace that comes from the victory we have in Christ.

REFLECTION QUESTIONS

1. Is it difficult to do the work the Lord has called you to when you don't receive recognition or reward?
2. How have you experienced God's blessings when you commit to serving Him with your whole heart?

PRAYER

O Lord, give Your blessing, we pray, to our daily work, that we may do it in faith and heartily, as to the Lord and not to men. All our powers of body and mind are Yours, and we devote them to Your service. Sanctify them, and the work in which we are engaged; and, Lord, so bless our efforts that they may bring forth in us the fruits of true wisdom.

Amen

-Thomas Arnold[1]

PHILIPPIANS 1.6

And I am sure of this, that he who began a good work in you will bring it to completion at the day of Jesus Christ.

If you've ever watched an artist do a live painting, you know that the finished product can look very different from the seemingly random strokes of color and texture that you see at the beginning. You might never guess the beautiful picture that eventually emerges from the swirls of paint. The same is true for us. We are God's masterpiece, but He isn't finished with us yet. He is still painting on the canvas of our lives. Don't be discouraged if you are not yet where you want to be. God is still at work in your life, but you won't see the finished version of yourself until you are with Christ.

God's work of sanctification in your life is not in vain! Each day, He is refining you, shaping you and building you through the power of the Holy Spirit so that you may live in victory. Embrace the beautiful new colors He is painting in your life and have faith that God is making you more like Him.

REFLECTION QUESTIONS

1. In what areas of your life has God begun a "good work"?
2. What areas of your life feel unfinished or needing more work?

PRAYER

Dear Father, thank You for the work You have already done in my life! You have graciously rescued me from darkness and placed my feet on solid ground. Continue to refine me by bringing to light things that I need to release, repent, and let go of so that I may live victoriously. Fill me with your Spirit that I may follow Your Word and serve You with my whole heart. Amen

PROVERBS 16.2-3

All a person's ways seem pure to them, but motives are weighed by the Lord. Commit to the Lord whatever you do, and He will establish your plans.

All too often we have seen spiritual leaders fall from grace because of sin. Most of these leaders did not start out to corrupt the Word of God or engage in sinful practices, but somewhere along the way, their motives changed. Their motives became less about God and more about their own personal agenda.

It is easy for us to think we are doing the right thing, but unless we are continually submitting our ways and our agendas to the Lord, we risk going astray. However, when we seek the Lord and commit to following Him with all of our heart, soul, and mind, He will guide us and establish our plans.

REFLECTION QUESTIONS

1. Think about a time when your own agenda got in the way of God's plan. What did you learn from that experience?
2. What current plans do you need to commit to the Lord?

PRAYER

Almighty God, our Help and Refuge, who knows that we can do nothing right without Your guidance and help; direct me by Your wisdom and power, that I may accomplish this task and, whatever I do according to your divine will, so that it may be beneficial to me and others to the glory of Your holy Name.
Amen
-Orthodox prayer[1]

2 TIMOTHY 4.7-8

I have fought the good fight, I have finished the race, I have kept the faith. Henceforth there is laid up for me the crown of righteousness, which the Lord, the righteous judge, will award to me on that day, and not only to me but also to all who have loved his appearing.

Sisters and brothers, we are still in the fight. We are still running the race set before us. Some of us are just past the starting line, others have been steadily pushing through for many miles. Keep going. Keep persevering. Keep your eyes on the Lord. We are not fighting in vain.

We know that we will be rewarded when we are united with Christ in heaven. On that glorious day, we will meet Him face to face. We will be greeted by our Lord, "Well done, good and faithful servant" (Matthew 25.21). Death is not the end—it is the beginning.

We need not fear coming to the end of the race. Victory awaits us: "'O death, where is your victory? O death, where is your sting?' the sting of death is sin, and the power of sin is the law. But thanks be to God, who gives us the victory through our Lord Jesus Christ" (1 Corinthians 15.55-57).

REFLECTION QUESTIONS

1. Where do you see yourself in "the race?"
2. How do you continue to persevere when life is difficult?
3. What are you most looking forward to when you reach heaven?

PRAYER

Heavenly Father,
Grant me the strength to fight the good fight of faith. Help me to keep my focus on You and lead me in the way I should go. May I keep my eyes on the prize—eternal life with You. Help me to cast my fears aside so I can run the race with perseverance—trusting You to provide.
Amen

1 CORINTHIANS 15.56–58

The sting of death is sin, and the power of sin is the law. But thanks be to God, who gives us the victory through our Lord Jesus Christ. Therefore, my beloved brothers, be steadfast, immovable, always abounding in the work of the Lord, knowing that in the Lord your labor is not in vain.

We have reached the end, and it is actually the beginning. The beginning of living fully into the victorious life we have in Jesus, the beginning of living life as His beloved, the beginning of walking a steadfast life grounded in Scripture, the beginning of partnering with Jesus to do His good works, and the beginning of knowing that the Kingdom labor we do is not in vain. This beginning, or for some a continuation, is rooted in the work of Jesus' death and resurrection. May we go forth and live in the victory we have through Christ Jesus.

REFLECTION QUESTIONS

As you conclude this book but continue your journey into victorious living, reflect on how these answers may have changed or grown:

1. What does victory through Jesus look like to you?
2. What does it mean to be beloved?
3. How are you steadfast?
4. What are the works of the Lord that you are to be abounding in?
5. How does it make you feel that your Kingdom labor will not be in vain?

PRAYER EXERCISE

1. Find a space with few distractions. This can be tough when you have children, a roommate, or live with family members. Go for a walk or sit in a car if you need to. Set a timer on your phone and do some breathing exercises. Breathe in deeply, and exhale. This will relax your body and begin to focus your mind on Jesus. Breathe in His truth. Breathe out your distractions, worries, and burdens.

2. Ask the Holy Spirit to guide this time with Jesus.

3. Speak one or all of these phrases to Jesus:
   Jesus, You are Victorious!
   Jesus, I am victorious through You.
   Jesus, we are victorious with You (This phrase will lead you to pray for a group of people: family, friends, co-workers, your church community).

4. As distractions come to mind, acknowledge them and refocus your breathing and attention to Jesus and the words you have chosen.

5. If you set a timer and think you need more time, if you can take it, do so. If not, thank Jesus for this time together.

Victorious Teaching Outline

THEME VERSE:

1 Corinthians 15.56-58
The sting of death is sin, and the power of sin is the law. 57 But thanks be to God, who gives us the victory through our Lord Jesus Christ. 58 Therefore, my beloved brothers, be steadfast, immovable, always abounding in the work of the Lord, knowing that in the Lord your labor is not in vain.

USING THESE OUTLINES:

The following teaching outlines are offered to help you communicate the central truth that the victorious life is rooted squarely in Christ's victory, without which no victory is available. We will explore our rich life—giving the theme through three teachings.

TEACHINGS:
1. Christ **Won** our Victory
2. We **Walk** in Christ's Victory
3. We **Work** in Christ's Victory

PREPARING TO TEACH THESE LESSONS:

1. Pray – Ask the Holy Spirit to guide you as you work through the material.
2. Read – Read carefully the passages offered in each outline.
3. Study – Study the texts deeply and completely.
4. Reflect – Sit with these texts meditating on the truth of God's Word.
5. Retreat – Share fellowship with the Lord seeking His guidance as to how you can use the material, and how He can use you to inspire, encourage, and strengthen the faith of those who will hear the teachings.

TEACHING OUTLINE #1

CHRIST WON OUR VICTORY - HE IS CHRIST THE VICTOR

Theme Verse:
1 Corinthians 15.56-58
[56]The sting of death is sin, and the power of sin is the law. [57]But thanks be to God, who gives us the victory through our Lord Jesus Christ. [58]Therefore, my beloved brothers, be steadfast, immovable, always abounding in the work of the Lord, knowing that in the Lord your labor is not in vain.

Key idea: No one wins alone.

I. Contact: The Myth of Me

The myth of me is to believe that I possess the power within myself to win the day. It is the false belief that all my victories are rooted in my own abilities, discipline, and efforts. We are conditioned by our culture:

- To believe primarily in ourselves
- To pull ourselves up by our bootstraps to depend only on ourselves
- To be self-reliant, self-willed, self-sufficient, and self-starters

It is easy to see the flaws of the myth of me if we consider teams (sports, families, or businesses). We understand that no one person is responsible for a team's success; not the quarterback, the dutiful child, the strong parent, or the inspirational business-minded visionary. Victories are always shared.

If we think deeply about so-called individual success stories (solo sport Olympians, the spelling bee champion, or the most well-known business leader), we may be tempted to think that those people are exceptions to the rule. However, every person who succeeds individually had someone in their life who encouraged, coached, mentored, taught, or in other ways helped the person become who they are.

Nowhere is the myth of me exposed more than in the Christian life. Although it is a popular notion among some believers that we must be good enough to earn and live a victorious life, the simplicity of the biblical message could not be any clearer. Our only victory is found in Christ.

II. Content: Christ Won our Victory – He is Christ the Victor

A. The resurrection of Christ is the central teaching of the Christian faith.

[3]For I delivered to you as of first importance what I also received: that Christ died for our sins in accordance with the Scriptures, [4]that he was buried, that he was raised on the third day in accordance with the Scriptures, [5]and that he appeared to Cephas, then to the twelve. [6]Then he appeared to more than five hundred brothers at one time, most of whom are still alive, though some have fallen asleep. [7]Then he appeared to James, then to all the apostles. [8]Last of all, as to one untimely born, he appeared also to me.
1 Corinthians 15.3-8

B. Without the resurrection there is no victory, hope, or forgiveness.

[12]Now if Christ is proclaimed as raised from the dead, how can some of you say that there is no resurrection of the dead? [13]But if there is no resurrection of the dead, then not even Christ has been raised. [14]And if Christ has not been raised, then our preaching is in vain and your faith is in vain. [15]We are even found to be misrepresenting God, because we testified about God that he raised Christ, whom he did not raise if it is true that the dead are not raised. **1 Corinthians 15.12-15**

C. Through His resurrection Christ won our victory.

[50]I tell you this, brothers: flesh and blood cannot inherit the kingdom of God, nor does the perishable inherit the imperishable. [51]Behold! I tell you a mystery. We shall not all sleep, but we shall all be changed, [52]in a moment, in the twinkling of an eye, at the last trumpet. For the trumpet will sound, and the dead will be raised imperishable, and we shall be changed. [53]For this perishable body must put on the imperishable, and this mortal body must put on immortality. [54]When the perishable puts on the imperishable, and the mortal puts on immortality, then shall come to pass the saying that is written: "Death is swallowed up in victory." [55]"O death, where is your victory? O death, where is your sting?"
1 Corinthians 15.50-55

"The Kingdom is inaugurated in Jesus as the Christus Victor, the One who overcomes through His Resurrection and Ascension."
—Dr. Don Davis[1]

III. Connection: Our victory is rooted in Christ's Victory

A. Our victory is rooted in the Victory of Christ.

1. He disarmed the rulers and authorities and put them to open shame, by triumphing over them in him. **Colossians 2.15**

2. [14]Since therefore the children share in flesh and blood, he himself likewise partook of the same

[1]Davis, Rev. Dr. Don L. The Kingdom of God, Module 2 (The Capstone Curriculum). TUMI / World Impact.

things, that through death he might destroy the one who has the power of death, that is, the devil, [15]and deliver all those who through fear of death were subject to lifelong slavery. **Hebrews 2.14-15**

3. The reason the Son of God appeared was to destroy the works of the devil. **1 John 3.8**

B. In Christ, the curse has been broken, salvation is offered, and we have the victory.

1. [13]Christ redeemed us from the curse of the law by becoming a curse for us—for it is written, "Cursed is everyone who is hanged on a tree"— [14]so that in Christ Jesus the blessing of Abraham might come to the Gentiles, so that we might receive the promised Spirit through faith. **Galatians 3.13-14**

2. [8]For by grace you have been saved through faith. And this is not your own doing; it is the gift of God, [9]not a result of works, so that no one may boast. **Ephesians 2.8-9**

3. [4]For everyone who has been born of God overcomes the world. And this is the victory that has overcome the world—our faith. [5]Who is it that overcomes the world except the one who believes that Jesus is the Son of God. **1 John 5.4-5**

The victorious life we experience was won for us by Christ our Lord. Christ is not just a champion or a victor...Christ is our Victor!

TEACHING OUTLINE #2
WE WALK IN CHRIST'S VICTORY

Theme Verse:
Corinthians 15.56-58
[56]The sting of death is sin, and the power of sin is the law. [57]But thanks be to God, who gives us the victory through our Lord Jesus Christ. [58]Therefore, my beloved brothers, be steadfast, immovable, always abounding in the work of the Lord, knowing that in the Lord your labor is not in vain.

Key idea: We never walk alone.

I. Contact: The dangers of individualized faith

The second most dangerous idea that threatens victorious living, beyond the myth of me, is the priority of the individualized Christian experience. It's the idea that my walk with Christ, and Christian victory, should be seen primarily through the lens of my personal experience with Christ while disregarding the need for biblical community. We are conditioned by culture:

- To see the world through a selfie lens
- To evaluate everything, including faith, in the context of self-realization
- To be self-actualized, self-evaluated, self-focused, and self-absorbed

In many circles, the emphasis on one's "personal relationship" with Jesus is promoted to the point of overshadowing the role and value of the local church. However, biblically, one's "personal relationship" with Christ and the local church are never mutually exclusive. An individualized experience, while certainly a part of one's relationship with the Lord, should never lead one to see the Christian life in a merely personalized fashion.

In a similar vein as our thinking of teams vs. individualized success, there is much to be gained from an understanding that the victories we share as Christians are just that–shared. No doubt Christians will experience victories in their individual lives; however, those victories should serve as testimonies to God's work and serve to promote and strengthen the faith of others.

Recognizing and sharing our victories together is crucial within the church. Testimonies of God's work in the lives of His people, and therefore the life of the church, serve not only as reminders of God's faithfulness and mighty acts, but also serve to encourage the church to expect the Lord to continue to provide the victory.

II. Content: The early church shared Christ's Victory together

A. They were edified when victories were shared

1. And they have conquered him by the blood of the Lamb and by the word of their testimony. **Revelation 12.11**

2. Therefore encourage one another and build one another up, just as you are doing. **1 Thessalonians 5.11**

B. They were encouraged in faith when victories were shared

1. [23]Let us hold fast the confession of our hope without wavering, for he who promised is faithful. [24]And let us consider how to stir up one another to love and good works, [25]not neglecting to meet together, as is the habit of some, but encouraging one another, and all the more as you see the Day drawing near. **Hebrews 10.23-25**

2. [8]Remember Jesus Christ, risen from the dead, the offspring of David, as preached in my gospel,

⁹for which I am suffering, bound with chains as a criminal. But the word of God is not bound! ¹⁰Therefore I endure everything for the sake of the elect, that they also may obtain the salvation that is in Christ Jesus with eternal glory. **2 Timothy 2.8-10**

C. They enjoyed rich fellowship when victories were shared

1. ⁴²And they devoted themselves to the apostles' teaching and the fellowship, to the breaking of bread and the prayers. ⁴³And awe came upon every soul, and many wonders and signs were being done through the apostles. ⁴⁴And all who believed were together and had all things in common. **Acts 2.42-44**

2. ¹That which was from the beginning, which we have heard, which we have seen with our eyes, which we looked upon and have touched with our hands, concerning the word of life— ²the life was made manifest, and we have seen it, and testify to it and proclaim to you the eternal life, which was with the Father and was made manifest to us— ³that which we have seen and heard we proclaim also to you, so that you too may have fellowship with us; and indeed our fellowship is with the Father and with his Son Jesus Christ. ⁴And we are writing these things so that our joy may be complete. **1 John 1.1-4**

We walk in victory together, not alone.
Our victories are shared in community.

III. Connection: We Walk in Christ's Victory together

A. We edify one another by sharing our victories

1. I will tell of your name to my brothers; in the midst of the congregation I will praise you. **Psalm 22.22**

2. Come and hear, all you who fear God, and I will tell what he has done for my soul. **Psalm 66.16**

3. Let those who delight in my righteousness shout for joy and be glad and say evermore, "Great is the Lord, who delights in the welfare of his servant!" 28 Then my tongue shall tell of your righteousness and of your praise all the day long. **Psalm 35.28**

B. We enjoy rich fellowship with each other by sharing our victories

1. And this is the testimony, that God gave us eternal life, and this life is in his Son. **1 John 5.11**

2. For I long to see you, that I may impart to you some spiritual gift to strengthen you— 12 that is, that we may be mutually encouraged by each other's faith, both yours and mine. **Romans 1.11-12**

3. Let the word of Christ dwell in you richly, teaching and admonishing one another in all wisdom, singing psalms and hymns and spiritual songs, with thankfulness in your hearts to God **Colossians 3.16**

Tell your story, for His glory! Your story may be the catalyst for others to believe in Jesus or to keep on believing.

TEACHING OUTLINE #3
WE WORK IN CHRIST'S VICTORY

Theme Verse:
1 Corinthians 15.56-58
[56]The sting of death is sin, and the power of sin is the law. [57]But thanks be to God, who gives us the victory through our Lord Jesus Christ. [58]Therefore, my beloved brothers, be steadfast, immovable, always abounding in the work of the Lord, knowing that in the Lord your labor is not in vain.

Key idea: We never work alone.

I. Contact: It don't come easy.

The third and perhaps most dangerous idea that threatens victorious living, is the notion that walking and working in Christ's victory should come easy. That believers naturally rise:

- To greet each new day on fire for the Lord
- Committed to the call of Christ on their lives and sharing their faith
- Ready to face any challenges that may come their way

Yet, as most experience life, the challenges of keeping and walking in a victorious mindset, commitment, and work firmly rooted in Christ's victory can be difficult. Some suggest that the difficulty is a reflection on what is believed, as if any effort spent to keep an idea is an indication that the idea is false. Some imply that if something doesn't come naturally it must be questionable.

However, every believer understands that there is work required to keep oneself grounded in victory and at work in the Lord. Paul offered the church in Corinth directives, a playbook, for this very battle. His words speak to keeping our minds, commitments, and work firmly rooted in Christ's victory.

Note that in our theme verse Paul is writing to the church expressed as "brethren," "beloved brothers," or "brothers and sisters" in various translations. This underscores the collective nature of the instructions. Though we all bear individual responsibility for our faith, commitments, and the work we do for the Lord, the work of living the victorious life is a shared work.

When grounded in a local fellowship of believers who encourage and support one another, the church works together to both cling to our victory in Christ and invite others to victory in Him.

II. Content: Three characteristics of the victorious life

A. Steadfast

1. This term relates to what is believed, a mindset, a firm faith. In this case, specifically the resurrection of Christ.

a. It is clear that some in the church at Corinth were teaching that Christ was not raised. **1 Corinthians 15.12**

b. Paul called the church to remain steadfast in their belief in the resurrection, and therefore their victory in Christ.

2. This term is used in other passages of what is believed, a mindset, a firm faith in other matters of faith.

a. But whoever is firmly established (steadfast) in his heart, being under no necessity but having his desire under control, and has determined this in his heart, to keep

her as his betrothed, he will do well.
1 Corinthians 7.37

b. [21]And you, who once were alienated
and hostile in mind, doing evil deeds,
[22]he has now reconciled in his body of flesh
by his death, in order to present you holy
and blameless and above reproach before
him, [23]if indeed you continue in the faith,
stable and steadfast, not shifting from the
hope of the gospel that you heard, which has
been proclaimed in all creation under
heaven, and of which I, Paul, became a
minister. **Colossians 1.21-23**

B. Immovable

1. This term speaks to external pressures, attacks,
temptations or persecution intended to dissuade
(move) believers from the truth of the resurrection.

a. The necessity of remaining immovable
rom external pressures is clear in Paul's
instruction, "Do not be deceived: 'Bad
company ruins good morals.'"
1 Corinthians 15.33

b. Paul called the church to remain
immovable in their commitment to the
victory rooted in the resurrection.

2. The attack on believers specifically over their faith
in and teachings about the resurrection of Christ,
and therefore their victory, is seen throughout the
New Testament. Two examples:

a. [2]Peter and James were arrested many

times for preaching the resurrection of the dead, for example: The Sadducees were "greatly annoyed because they were teaching the people and proclaiming in Jesus the resurrection from the dead. ³And they arrested them and put them in custody until the next day, for it was already evening." **Acts 4.2-3**

b. Paul was also arrested many times for teaching the resurrection, for example: "It is with respect to the resurrection of the dead that I am on trial before you this day." **Acts 24.21**

C. Abounding in the work of the Lord

1. This phrase speaks to the bountiful, fruitful, and dedicated work in the Lord done to advance the Kingdom rooted in Christ's victory.

a. For so the Lord has commanded us, saying, "I have made you a light for the Gentiles, that you may bring salvation to the ends of the earth." **Acts 14.47**

b. Declare his glory among the nations, his marvelous works among all the peoples! **1 Chronicles 16.24**

2. Christ's victory, demonstrated in His resurrection and ascension, was the central message of the Good News (the Gospel).

a. ³I delivered to you as of first importance what I also received: that Christ died for our sins in accordance with the Scriptures, ⁴that

he was buried, that he was raised on
the third day in accordance with the
Scriptures. **1 Corinthians 15.3-4**

b. For I am not ashamed of the gospel, for it
is the power of God for salvation to everyone
who believes, to the Jew first and also to the
Greek. **Romans 1.16**

*Let us hold fast the confession of our hope without wavering,
for he who promised is faithful. Hebrews 10.23*

III. Connection: We work in Christ's Victory

**A. We are a community of victors who work to encourage
faith in others by walking in and sharing our victories.**

1. Oh give thanks to the Lord; call upon his name;
make known his deeds among the peoples!
Psalm 105.1

2. ¹Oh give thanks to the Lord, for he is good, for his
steadfast love endures forever! ²Let the redeemed of
the Lord say so. **Psalm 107.1-2**

3. In order that the Gentiles might glorify God for
his mercy. As it is written, "Therefore I will praise
you among the Gentiles, and sing to your name."
Romans 15.9

**B. We are a community of victors who work together to
invite others into the victory found only in Christ.**

1. ¹You then, my child, be strengthened by the grace
that is in Christ Jesus, ²and what you have heard

from me in the presence of many witnesses entrust to faithful men, who will be able to teach others also. **2 Timothy 2.1-2**

2. [3]Praise be to the God and Father of our Lord Jesus Christ! In his great mercy he has given us new birth into a living hope through the resurrection of Jesus Christ from the dead, [4]and into an inheritance that can never perish, spoil or fade. This inheritance is kept in heaven for you, [5]who through faith are shielded by God's power until the coming of the salvation that is ready to be revealed in the last time. **1 Peter 1.3-5**

3. [9]But you are a chosen race, a royal priesthood, a holy nation, a people for his own possession, that you may proclaim the excellencies of him who called you out of darkness into his marvelous light. [10]Once you were not a people, but now you are God's people; once you had not received mercy, but now you have received mercy. **1 Peter 2.9-10**

C. We are a community of victors who work knowing our labor is not in vain.

1. [10]At the name of Jesus every knee should bow, in heaven and on earth and under the earth, [11]and every tongue confess that Jesus Christ is Lord, to the glory of God the Father. **Philippians 2.10-11**

2. Behold, he is coming with the clouds, and every eye will see him, even those who pierced him, and all tribes of the earth will wail on account of him. Even so. Amen. **Revelation 1.7**

3. [50]I tell you this, brothers: flesh and blood cannot inherit the kingdom of God, nor does the perishable

inherit the imperishable. [51]Behold! I tell you a mystery. We shall not all sleep, but we shall all be changed, [52]in a moment, in the twinkling of an eye, at the last trumpet. For the trumpet will sound, and the dead will be raised imperishable, and we shall be changed. [53]For this perishable body must put on the imperishable, and this mortal body must put on immortality. [54]When the perishable puts on the imperishable, and the mortal puts on immortality, then shall come to pass the saying that is written: "Death is swallowed up in victory." [55]"O death, where is your victory? O death, where is your sting?" **1 Corinthians 15.50-55**

Let us encourage one another as we work in Christ's victory! Let us remain "steadfast, immovable, always abounding in the work of the Lord, knowing that in the Lord your labor is not in vain."
1 Corinthians 15.58

INFORMATION ON WORLD IMPACT

World Impact empowers urban leaders and partners with local churches to reach their cities with the Gospel.

Empower
We believe the hope of the Gospel in our cities lies with training, equipping, and empowering Kingdom-minded leaders to fulfill the vision the Holy Spirit has given them to accomplish through their local church.

Partner
The Gospel is already alive and active in our cities. We simply want to work with denominations, ministry networks, and local church leaders who are already effective for even more Kingdom impact.

Reach
We believe that if we reach the city, we will reach the world. As we expand into increasingly multicultural U.S. cities, we have an incredible opportunity to grow the reach of the Gospel through new disciples who have direct ties to their country of origin.

Learn more at *worldimpact.org*

WORLD IMPACT URBAN LEADERSHIP RETREATS

Our mission is to empower urban leaders and partner with local churches to reach their cities with the gospel by offering retreats that equip women and men to be leaders in their homes, churches, and communities.

Our values:

- **Empowerment**: We are passionate about empowering men and women to discover, develop, and demonstrate their calling to ministry within the body of Christ and beyond (Acts 1.8).

- **Community**: We believe Christians are called to community. In community we build each other up recognizing individual God-given gifts and talents and joining together to expand the Kingdom (Hebrews 10.24-25).

- **Church-Centered**: We emphasize the one Church that Jesus built consists of all believers globally who gather in neighborhoods as local expressions of that church (Matthew 16.19 | Acts 2.44-47).

- **Multiplication**: We desire to empower leaders and churches to conduct retreats in their communities by resourcing through training materials and modeling (2 Timothy 2.2).

Our culture:

In all we say and do, we desire to glorify Christ and make Him known. We seek to create a loving and caring environment that welcomes individuals from all backgrounds and ethnic groups. We desire that individuals who attend our retreats experience a sense of belonging to a larger community.

Authors

Rev. Hope Flask is a wife, mother, worship leader, song writer, and senior pastor of Outside The Walls Church and Ministries. She along with her husband, Tim, planted Outside the Walls to be a place for the poor, broken, and oppressed. Both have experienced being thrown away and thought they were forever lost until Jesus came and turned what the world called trash into a treasure.

Damon Owens is the Sr. Pastor of Genesis Church-Antioch; a vibrant multigenerational church community that is committed to local missions and sharing the Gospel to low- and moderate-income families within the city and surrounding areas. He is a Ministry Developer for World Impact, the Chairman of the Board of Overseers for Converge PacWest, and plays an active role in the DeVos Urban Leadership Initiative. He is also pursuing his Master's Degree in Organizational and Leadership Development. He loves golf, Formula One Racing and is a loyal Las Vegas Raiders fan. He is married to Shantell, has three daughters and five beautiful grandchildren: Christian, Anaiyah, Gia, Olivia, and Derrick Jr.

 **Kim Contreras** heard the call to urban America while a student at John Brown University. She joined the World Impact Fresno team in 1993. During her time on staff, it has been a deep honor to learn about the city from her neighbors and friends by living in the Lowell and Hidalgo communities, participating in Bible clubs, church plants, and street outreach to survivors of human trafficking. Her most recent role as Ministry Developer focuses on Trauma Healing and Retreats. She can be found on Bond St. with her husband Manuel and their two children, Ian (17) and Sophia (12), sharing an Anaconda burrito from Yareli's, enjoying good coffee, and playing with their cats: Fuego, Sombra, and Rosa.

 **Pastor Darnell Bryant** has been happily married to Abigail Bryant for ten years. He has an amazing two-year-old son, Azel. Pastor Darnell is the Director of Operations for the Union Rescue Mission in Wichita, KS. He has pastored with Mending Place for 6 years. Pastor Darnell had 6 years of experience as a youth minister before becoming an Associate Pastor. He pastored a successful restorative ministry that has led those that were broken into healing. Pastor Darnell enjoys spending time eating out with family and friends at local restaurants.

 **Rev. Ted Smith** currently serves as Executive Assistant to the National Director of Church Planting and Head Dean of the Evangel School of Urban Church Planting for World Impact. He also serves as Dean of The Urban Ministry Institute (TUMI) of Dallas and as Pastor of Southwood Church in Greenville, TX. He holds a B.A. in Ministry and Leadership from Dallas Christian College, an M.A. in New Testament and Preaching from Johnson University, and an M.A. in Global Leadership from Dallas Baptist University. Ted's passion is to develop and equip leaders for the work of ministry through coaching, mentoring, conferences, seminars, and classroom instruction. Ted and his wife live in Rowlett, TX. They have three children and nine grandchildren.

 **Tina Busenitz** is the Director of Retreats and Strategic Hiring for World Impact. She oversees all the Urban Leadership Retreats as well as serving as director of the Wichita Women's Retreat. Tina has served as a missionary with World Impact for 18 years, along with her husband, Daren. They have ministered in a variety of roles, including planting two churches— one in 2002 and one in 2008. Her passion is empowering women of God. She obtained her B.A. in Sociology from Wichita State University and is currently pursuing her Master's Degree in Communications from Wichita State. Daren and Tina reside in Wichita, Kansas, and have three sons, Jackson, Justus and Caden. Contact: tbusenitz@worldimpact.org

 **Candy Gibson** has been a missionary with World Impact since 2006. During that time she has had the honor of being a church planter, youth leader, camp counselor, an incarnational missionary, and now is part of the Trauma Healing team. Oh, and she loves coffee, art, biblical feminism and Parks and Rec.

Made in the USA
Monee, IL
09 September 2022

13690718R00057